PERFECT
ROASTS

Consultant Editor:
Valerie Ferguson

LORENZ BOOKS

Contents

Introduction

A roast is always special. Even families whose busy schedules prevent them from sharing meals very often somehow manage to find time to gather round the table for a roast. Worldwide it is the centrepiece of high days and holidays from Thanksgiving turkey in the United States to Easter Sunday spit-roast lamb in Greece.

Roasting best suits larger cuts of meat which remain succulent inside while crisp on the outside. Smaller cuts tend to dry out and shrivel. The quality of the meat is crucial to success. Opinion is divided about whether it is better to roast on or off the bone. Meat is generally thought to have a better flavour if it is cooked on the bone, but boneless cuts are certainly easier to carve.

Although roasting takes quite a long time, once a few basics have been mastered, it is one of the easiest ways of cooking meat and poultry. The following pages contain all you need to know about types of chicken, suitable cuts of meat, roasting times, how to tell if meat is ready and making gravy. The recipes range from basic but satisfying family roasts to more elaborate and extravagant dinner party dishes. Whatever the occasion you are sure to find the perfect roast.

Types of Chicken

A fresh chicken should have a plump breast and the skin should be creamy in colour. The tip of the breast bone should be pliable.

Roasters

These birds are about six to twelve months old and weigh 1.5–2 kg/ 3–4½ lb. They will feed a family.

Corn-fed Chickens

These are free-range birds and are generally more expensive. They usually weigh 1.2–1.5 kg/2½–3 lb.

Spring Chickens

These birds are about three months old and weigh 900 g–1.2 kg/2–2½ lb. They will serve three to four people.

Poussins

These are four to six weeks old and weigh 450–675 g/1–1½ lb. One poussin makes one serving.

Double Poussins

These are eight to ten weeks old and weigh 800–900 g/1¾–2 lb. They will serve two people and may be oven-roasted or pot-roasted.

COOK'S TIP: A frozen chicken should be thawed slowly. Never use hot water, as this will make it tough.

Roasting Times for Poultry

Note: Cooking times given here are for unstuffed birds. For stuffed birds, add 20 minutes to the total cooking time.

Poussin: 450–675 g/1–1½ lb
 1–1¼ hours at 180°C/350°F/Gas 4
Chicken: 1.2–1.5 kg/2½–3 lb
 1–1¼ hours at 190°C/375°F/Gas 5
1.5–1.75 kg/3½–4 lb
 1¼–1¾ hours at 190°C/375°F/Gas 5
2–2.25 kg/4½–5 lb
 1½–2 hours at 190°C/375°F/Gas 5
Pheasant: 800 g–1.2 kg/1¾–2½ lb
 1–1¼ hours at 180°C/350°F/Gas 4
Duck: 1.5–2.25 kg/3–5 lb
 1¾–2¼ hours at 200°C/400°F/Gas 6
Turkey: 2.75–3.6 kg/6–8 lb
 3–3½ hours at 160°C/325°F/Gas 3
3.6–5.4 kg/8–12 lb
 3–4 hours at 160°C/325°F/Gas 3
5.4–7.2 kg/12–16 lb
 4–5 hours at 160°C/325°F/Gas 3

Stuffing tips

• Use cool, not hot or chilled stuffing.
• Pack it loosely because it expands.
• Cook left-over stuffing in a separate dish.
• Do not stuff poultry until just before roasting.
• Do not stuff the body cavity of a large bird.

Types of Meat for Roasting

Whatever the type, prime quality meat is best for roasting, but some less expensive cuts are perfect for pot roasts.

Beef

Fore rib, middle rib, wing or prime rib, middle rib, fillet, sirloin, aitchbone are ideal for roasting. Brisket, silverside, thick flank or top rump and topside are all good for pot-roasting.

Veal

Shoulder or oyster, best end of neck, loin, fillet, breast, leg, topside or cushion.

Lamb

Shoulder, best end of neck or rack, saddle, loin, breast, leg or gigot (whole or divided into leg fillet and knuckle or shank).

Pork

Shoulder (spare rib), blade, hind loin, tenderloin, leg (whole or divided into fillet and knuckle or hough), belly, spare ribs. Also gammon joints and bacon collar and hock. Hand and spring are good for pot-roasting.

Roasting Times for Meat

The times apply to meat roasted at 180°C/350°F/Gas 4.

Beef:

rare	675–900 g/1½–2 lb	50 minutes–1 hour
	900 g–1.5 kg/2–3½ lb	1–1½ hours
medium	675–900 g/1½–2 lb	1–1½ hours
	900 g–1.5 kg/2–3½ lb	1½–2 hours
well done	675–900 g/1½–2 lb	1¼–1½ hours
	900 g–1.5 kg/2–3½ lb	2–2½ hours

Veal:

	675–900 g/1½–2 lb	1–1½ hours
	900 g–1.5 kg/2–3½ lb	1½–2 hours

Lamb:

medium	675–900 g/1½–2 lb	50 minutes–1 hour
	900 g–1.5 kg/2–3½ lb	1–1½ hours
well done	675–900 g/1½–2 lb	1–1½ hours
	900 g–1.5 kg/2–3½ lb	1½–2 hours

Pork:

	675–900 g/1½–2 lb	1½–1¾ hours
	900 g–1.5 kg/2–3½ lb	1¾–2¾ hours

Techniques

Browning Meat

Large joints are sometimes seared first, either by roasting briefly at a high temperature and then reducing the heat or by frying.

1 Frying the meat dry. Heat a little oil until it is very hot, then fry the meat over a high heat until it is well browned on all surfaces. Turn it using two spatulas or spoons.

2 If roasting, transfer the meat, in its roasting tin, to the oven. If pot-roasting, add a small amount of liquid and cover the pan tightly.

Testing When Meat is Cooked

The cooking times given in a recipe are guidelines. The shape of a cut affects how long it takes to cook, and people have different preferences, so testing is essential.

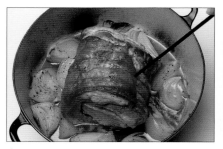

1 Large joints can be tested with a metal skewer. Insert it into the thickest part. After 30 seconds withdraw it. If it is warm, the meat is rare; if it is hot, the meat is well cooked.

2 The most reliable test is with a meat thermometer inserted in the centre of the joint away from bones. Some instant-read thermometers are inserted at the end of cooking. Follow manufacturer's instructions.

Pot-roasting

This method of cooking tenderizes tougher cuts. Prime cuts can also be pot-roasted, but cooking times are shorter. Meat to be pot-roasted may or may not have an initial searing.

Natural Law of Roasting

A joint will continue to cook in retained heat for 5–10 minutes after being removed from the oven or pot, so it is a good idea to take it out when it is just below the desired thermometer reading.

Resting a Joint Before Carving

Once a joint is removed from the oven or pot, it should be transferred to a carving board and left in a warm place to rest for 10–15 minutes. It can be covered with a loose tent of cooking foil, but air should be allowed to circulate. The joint will retain its heat and, during this time, as the temperature evens out, the flesh reabsorbs most of the juices. Thus the juices won't leak during carving. While the meat is resting is a good time to make the gravy from the juices in the roasting tin.

Making Gravy

Gravy made from the roasting juices is rich in flavour and colour. It is a traditional accompaniment for roast meat and poultry.

1 Spoon off most of the fat from the roasting tin. Set the tin over a moderately high heat. When the juices begin to sizzle, add flour and stir to combine well.

2 Cook, scraping the tin well to mix in all the residue until the mixture forms a smooth brown paste. Add stock or other liquid as specified and bring to the boil, stirring constantly. Simmer until thickened, then season with salt and pepper.

Roast Chicken with Lemon & Herbs

A well-flavoured chicken is essential for this subtle roast – use a free-range or corn-fed bird, if possible.

Serves 4

INGREDIENTS
1.5 kg/3–3½ lb chicken
1 unwaxed lemon, halved
small bunch fresh thyme sprigs
1 bay leaf
15 g/½ oz/1 tbsp butter, softened
60–90 ml/4–6 tbsp chicken stock
  or water
salt and ground black pepper

1 Preheat the oven to 200°C/400°F/ Gas 6. Season the chicken inside and out with salt and pepper.

2 Squeeze the juice of one lemon half and then place the juice, the squeezed lemon half, the thyme and bay leaf in the chicken cavity. Tie the legs with string and rub the breast with butter.

COOK'S TIP: Be sure to save the carcasses of roast poultry for stock. Freeze them until you have several, then place in a large casserole dish, cover with water and simmer gently for 2 hours with vegetables, such as carrots, leeks, onions and aromatic herbs such as bay and chives.

3 Place the chicken on a rack in a roasting tin. Squeeze over the juice of the other lemon half. Roast the chicken for 1 hour, basting two or three times, until the juices run clear when the thickest part of the thigh is pierced with a knife.

4 Pour the juices from the cavity into the roasting tin and transfer the chicken to a carving board. Cover loosely with foil and leave to stand for 10–15 minutes before carving.

5 Meanwhile, skim off the fat from the cooking juices. Add the stock or water and boil over a medium heat, stirring and scraping the base of the pan, until slightly reduced. Strain and serve with the chicken.

Whisky Chicken with Onion Marmalade

An unusual whisky-flavoured paste on roasted chicken portions.

Serves 4

INGREDIENTS
25 g/1 oz/2 tbsp sesame seeds, crushed
2 garlic cloves, crushed
pinch of paprika
30 ml/2 tbsp oil
30 ml/2 tbsp whisky
30 ml/2 tbsp clear honey
4 chicken portions
salt and ground black pepper

FOR THE MARMALADE
30 ml/2 tbsp oil
2 large onions, finely sliced
1 green (bell) pepper, seeded
   and sliced
150 ml/¼ pint/⅔ cup vegetable stock

1 Preheat the oven to 190°C/375°F/Gas 5. In a small bowl, make a paste with the sesame seeds, garlic, paprika, oil, whisky and honey. Season with salt and pepper.

2 Slit the chicken skins and spread in the paste. Roast for 40 minutes.

3 Meanwhile, make the onion marmalade. Heat the oil in a frying pan and fry the onion slices over a medium-high heat for 15 minutes. Add the green pepper and fry for 5 minutes more. Stir in the stock, season with salt and pepper and cook gently, stirring occasionally, for about 20 minutes. Serve warm with the cooked chicken.

Spicy Roast Chicken

The chicken is opened out and marinated in a mixture of lemon juice, herbs and spices before roasting.

Serves 4

INGREDIENTS
1.5 kg/3–3½ lb chicken
juice of 1 lemon
4 garlic cloves, finely chopped
15 ml/1 tbsp each cayenne pepper, paprika, dried oregano
10 ml/2 tsp olive oil
salt and ground black pepper
sprigs of fresh coriander (cilantro), to garnish
mixed sliced peppers, to serve

1 Cut the backbone from the chicken and turn it over. With the heel of your hand, press down and break the breastbone. Open the chicken out flat. Insert a skewer through the thighs to keep it flat during cooking.

2 Place the chicken in a shallow dish and pour over the lemon juice.

3 Combine the garlic, cayenne, paprika, oregano, black pepper and oil and rub evenly over the chicken. Cover and leave to marinate for 2–3 hours at room temperature.

4 Preheat the oven to 200°C/400°F/Gas 6. Season both sides of the chicken with salt and place it, skin side up, in a shallow roasting tin. Roast, basting with the juices in the tin, for 1 hour, or until the juices run clear when the thickest part of the thigh is pierced with the point of a knife. Garnish with fresh coriander sprigs and serve with mixed sliced peppers.

Chicken with Wild Mushrooms & Garlic

The country-fresh flavour of wild mushrooms with just a hint of herbs makes a refreshingly different roast.

Serves 4

INGREDIENTS
45 ml/3 tbsp olive or vegetable oil
1.5 kg/3–3½ lb chicken
1 large onion, finely chopped
3 celery sticks, chopped
2 garlic cloves, crushed
275 g/10 oz/4 cups fresh wild mushrooms,
  sliced if large
5 ml/1 tsp chopped fresh thyme
250 ml/8 fl oz/1 cup chicken stock
250 ml/8 fl oz/1 cup dry white wine
juice of 1 lemon
30 ml/2 tbsp chopped fresh parsley
120 ml/4 fl oz/½ cup sour cream
salt and ground black pepper
flat leaf parsley, to garnish
fresh green beans, to serve

1 Preheat the oven to 190°C/375°F/ Gas 5. Heat the oil in a roasting tin and brown the chicken all over.

COOK'S TIP: Wild mushrooms must be cleaned well to remove any grit. Brush gently with a dry brush or a damp cloth. Do not wash them as they will retain the water and become soggy. As a substitute, use cultivated mushrooms instead.

2 Add the onion and fry for about 2-3 minutes. Add the celery, garlic, mushrooms and thyme and cook for 3 minutes.

3 Pour the stock, wine and lemon juice into the roasting tin. Sprinkle over half of the parsley and season well. Roast the chicken and vegetables for 1½–1¾ hours, or until tender, basting occasionally.

4 Remove the chicken from the roasting tin and keep warm. Put the roasting tin on the hob and stir in the soured cream over a gentle heat, adding a little extra stock or water if necessary to make the juices into a thick pouring sauce.

5 Arrange the chicken on a plate, surrounded by the creamy mushrooms. Garnish with parsley sprigs and serve the chicken with the sauce and fresh green beans.

Roast Chicken with Almonds

Stuffed with a lightly spiced mixture of couscous, fruit and nuts, this Moroccan-style roast is full of flavour.

Serves 4

INGREDIENTS
1.5 kg/3–3½ lb chicken
pinch of ground ginger
pinch of ground cinnamon
pinch of saffron, dissolved in 30 ml/2 tbsp
    boiling water
2 onions, chopped
300 ml/½ pint/1¼ cups chicken stock
45 g/1½ oz/3 tbsp flaked almonds
10 g/¼ oz/1 tbsp plain (all-purpose) flour
salt and ground black pepper
lemon wedges and fresh coriander (cilantro),
    to garnish

FOR THE STUFFING
50 g/2 oz/⅓ cup couscous
120 ml/4 fl oz/½ cup chicken stock, boiling
20 g/¾ oz/1½ tbsp butter
1 shallot, finely chopped
½ small cooking apple
25 g/1 oz/2 tbsp flaked (sliced) almonds
25 g/1 oz/2 tbsp ground almonds
30 ml/2 tbsp chopped fresh coriander
    (cilantro)
pinch of paprika
pinch of cayenne pepper

1 Preheat the oven to 180°C/350°F/ Gas 4. Prepare the stuffing. Place the couscous in a bowl and pour in the stock. Stir and set aside for 10 minutes. Melt the butter in a frying pan and fry the shallot for 2–3 minutes, until soft.

2 Fluff up the couscous and stir in the shallot and the butter from the pan. Peel, core and chop the apple and add to the couscous with the remaining stuffing ingredients. Season and stir well.

3 Loosely push the couscous mixture into the neck end of the chicken and truss or secure the neck with cocktail sticks. Blend the ginger and cinnamon with the saffron water. Rub the chicken with salt and pepper and then pour over the saffron water.

4 Place the chicken in a small roasting tin. Spoon the onions and stock around the edge and cover the dish with foil, pinching it around the edges of the dish. Cook for 1¼ hours, then increase the oven temperature to 200°C/400°F/Gas 6.

5 Transfer the chicken to a plate and strain the cooking liquid into a jug, reserving the onions. Return the chicken to the roasting tin with the onions, baste with a little of the cooking liquid and scatter with the almonds. Return to the oven and cook for about 30 minutes, until the chicken is golden brown and cooked through.

6 Pour off the fat from the reserved cooking juices and pour into a small saucepan. Blend the flour with 30 ml/ 2 tbsp cold water, stir into the pan with the cooking juices and heat gently, stirring to make a smooth sauce. Garnish the chicken with lemon wedges and coriander and serve with the sauce.

Stuffed Spring Chickens

This dish is widely found in the Middle East. The stuffing is a delicious blend of meat, nuts and rice and makes a great dinner party dish.

Serves 6–8

INGREDIENTS
2 x 1 kg/2¼ lb chickens
15 g/½ oz/1 tbsp butter

FOR THE STUFFING
45 ml/3 tbsp vegetable oil
1 onion, chopped
450 g/1 lb/4 cups minced (ground) lamb
75 g/3 oz/¾ cup almonds, chopped
75 g/3 oz/¾ cup pine nuts
350 g/12 oz/2 cups cooked rice
salt and ground black pepper
fresh mint, to garnish

1 Preheat the oven to 180°C/350°F/ Gas 4. Rinse the body cavities of the chickens in cold water.

2 Heat the oil in a large frying pan and sauté the onion until slightly softened. Add the minced lamb and cook over a moderate heat, stirring frequently, for 4–8 minutes, until well browned. Set aside.

3 Heat a small pan over a moderate heat and dry fry the almonds and pine nuts for 2–3 minutes, until golden, shaking the pan frequently.

4 Mix together the meat mixture, chopped almonds, pine nuts and cooked rice. Season with salt and freshly ground black pepper, then spoon the mixture into the body cavities of the chickens. Rub the chickens all over with the butter.

5 Place the chickens in a large roasting dish, cover with foil and bake in the oven for 45–60 minutes. After 30 minutes, remove the foil and baste the chickens with the pan juices.

6 Continue cooking without the foil until the chickens are cooked through and the meat juices run clear when the thickest part of the thigh is pierced with the point of a knife. Serve the roast chickens, cut into portions, garnished with fresh mint.

Roast Turkey with Mushrooms

Roast turkey can taste disappointing, but stuffing it with wild mushrooms boosts both flavour and succulence.

Serves 6–8

INGREDIENTS
5 kg/10 lb turkey
butter, for basting
watercress, to garnish

FOR THE MUSHROOM STUFFING
50 g/2 oz/4 tbsp unsalted butter
1 medium onion, chopped
225 g/8 oz/3 cups wild mushrooms,
    trimmed and chopped
75 g/3 oz/1½ cups fresh white breadcrumbs
115 g/4 oz pork sausages, skinned
1 small fresh truffle, sliced (optional)
5 drops truffle oil (optional)
salt and ground black pepper

FOR THE GRAVY
15 g/½ oz/¼ cup dried ceps, soaked
75 ml/5 tbsp medium sherry
400 ml/14 fl oz/1⅔ cups
    chicken stock
20 ml/4 tsp cornflour (cornstarch)
5 ml/1 tsp Dijon mustard
2.5 ml/½ tsp wine vinegar
salt and ground black pepper
knob of butter

1 Preheat the oven to 220°C/425°F/ Gas 7. To make the stuffing, melt the butter in a saucepan, add the onion and fry gently without colouring. Add the mushrooms and stir until their juices begin to flow.

2 Remove from the heat, add the breadcrumbs, sausage meat and the truffle and truffle oil, if using. Season and stir well to combine.

3 Spoon the stuffing into the neck cavity of the turkey and enclose, fastening the skin on the underside with a skewer.

4 Rub the skin of the turkey with butter, place in a large roasting tin and roast for 50 minutes. Lower the temperature to 180°C/350°F/Gas 4 and cook for a further 2½ hours.

5 Transfer the turkey to a carving board, cover loosely with foil and keep warm. To make the gravy, spoon off the fat from the roasting tin. Heat the remaining liquid until reduced to a sediment. Drain and finely chop the ceps. Add the ceps to the roasting tin with the sherry and stir briskly to loosen the sediment. Stir in the chicken stock.

6 Blend the cornflour and mustard with 10 ml/2 tsp water and the wine vinegar. Stir into the juices in the tin and simmer to thicken. Season with salt and pepper and stir in a knob of butter.

7 Garnish the turkey with bunches of watercress. Pour the gravy into a serving jug and serve separately.

Roast Duckling with Honey

A sweet-and-sour orange sauce is the perfect foil for this rich-tasting
Polish duck recipe, and frying the orange rind intensifies the flavour.

Serves 4

INGREDIENTS
2.25 kg/5 lb oven-ready duckling
2.5 ml/½ tsp ground allspice
1 orange
15 ml/1 tbsp sunflower oil
15 g/½ oz/2 tbsp plain (all-purpose) flour
150 ml/¼ pint/⅔ cup chicken or
 duck stock
10 ml/2 tsp red wine vinegar
15 ml/1 tbsp clear honey
salt and ground black pepper
watercress and thinly pared orange rind,
 to serve

1 Preheat the oven to 220°C/425°F/
Gas 7. Using a fork, pierce the
duckling all over, taking care to avoid
the breast, so that the fat runs out
during cooking.

2 Rub all over the skin of the
duckling with allspice and sprinkle
with salt and pepper.

3 Put the duckling on a rack over a
roasting tin and cook for about
20 minutes. Reduce the oven
temperature to 190°C/375°F/Gas 5,
and cook for a further 2 hours.

4 Meanwhile, thinly pare the rind
from the orange and cut into very fine
strips. Heat the oil in a pan and gently
fry the orange rind for 2–3 minutes.
Squeeze the juice from the orange and
set aside.

5 Transfer the duckling to a warmed
serving dish and keep warm. Drain off
all but 30 ml/2 tbsp fat from the tin,
sprinkle in the flour and stir well.

6 Stir in the chicken or duck stock,
red wine vinegar, honey, orange juice
and rind. Bring to the boil, stirring.
Simmer for 2–3 minutes. Season
the sauce and serve the duckling
with watercress and thinly pared
orange rind.

Roast Pheasant with Juniper Berries

Fresh sage and juniper berries are often used in Italian cooking to flavour pheasant and other game.

Serves 3–4

INGREDIENTS
1.2–1.4 kg/2½–3 lb pheasant, with liver
   finely chopped (optional)
45 ml/3 tbsp olive oil
2 sprigs of fresh sage
3 shallots, chopped
1 bay leaf
2 lemon quarters, plus 5 ml/1 tsp juice
30 g/1¼ oz/2 tbsp juniper berries,
   lightly crushed
4 thin slices pancetta or bacon
90 ml/6 tbsp dry white wine
250 ml/8 fl oz/1 cup hot chicken stock
25 g/1 oz/2 tbsp butter, at room temperature
30 ml/2 tbsp plain (all-purpose) flour
30 ml/2 tbsp brandy
salt and ground black pepper
sage leaves, to garnish

1 Wash the pheasant under cool water. Drain and pat dry with kitchen paper. Rub with 15 ml/1 tbsp of the olive oil. Place the remaining oil, sage leaves, shallots, and bay leaf in a shallow bowl. Add the lemon juice and juniper berries. Place the pheasant and lemon quarters in the bowl with the marinade and spoon it over the bird. Marinate for several hours in a cool place, turning the pheasant occasionally. Remove the lemon.

2 Preheat the oven to 180°C/350°F/Gas 4. Place the pheasant in a roasting tin, reserving the marinade. Sprinkle the cavity with salt and pepper and place the bay leaf inside.

3 Arrange some of the sage leaves on the breast of the pheasant and lay the pancetta or bacon over the top. Secure with string.

4 Spoon the remaining marinade and wine on top of the pheasant and roast until tender, about 30 minutes per 450 g/1 lb. Baste frequently with the cooking juices. Transfer the pheasant to a warmed serving platter, discarding the string and pancetta.

5 Skim off any surface fat from the cooking juices and pour in the stock, scraping the tin. Add the liver, if using, and bring to the boil. Cook for 2–3 minutes and strain into a saucepan.

6 Blend the butter to a paste with the flour. Stir into the gravy, a little at a time. Boil for 2–3 minutes, stirring to smooth out any lumps. Remove from the heat, stir in the brandy and serve, garnished with sage leaves.

Fig-stuffed Pork with Brandy

Pork stuffed with dried fruit and spiked with brandy makes a sophisticated and elegant dinner party dish.

Serves 4

INGREDIENTS
1 large pork fillet, about 500 g/
   1¼ lb, trimmed
45 ml/3 tbsp brandy
30 ml/2 tbsp chopped fresh herbs, such as
   parsley, dill or chives
8 dried figs, halved
oil, for brushing
15 ml/1 tbsp plain (all-purpose) flour
300 ml/½ pint/1¼ cups pork or
   chicken stock
salt and ground black pepper
sprigs of fresh parsley,
   to garnish

2 Fold the meat over the filling and tie with raffia or string. Put the pork into a roasting tin, brush with oil, season with pepper and roast for 35 minutes.

1 Preheat the oven to 190°C/375°F/Gas 5. Cut a deep slit along the length of the pork fillet, but do not cut all the way through. Open it out and brush with 15 ml/1 tbsp of the brandy. Sprinkle the herbs over and season with salt and pepper. Arrange the dried fig halves in a row on top of the fillet.

3 Lift the meat from the roasting tin and keep it hot. Spoon off the excess fat, leaving the sediment and about 15 ml/1 tbsp of the fat in the base of the tin. Place the tin on the hob over a medium heat.

VARIATION: This recipe also works very well with dry sherry, Noilly Prat or Madeira.

4 Stir in the flour and cook for 1 minute, then whisk in the stock and remaining brandy. Cook until thickened, then boil for 2 minutes, whisking frequently. Season with salt and pepper to taste.

5 Slice the meat, garnish with parsley sprigs and serve with the gravy.

Roast Loin of Pork with Apple Stuffing

Pork and apple is a classic combination the world over. This succulent stuffed loin is based on a Russian recipe.

Serves 6–8

INGREDIENTS
1.75 kg/4–4½ lb boned loin of pork
300 ml/½ pint/1¼ cups dry cider
150 ml/¼ pint/⅔ cup sour cream
7.5 ml/1½ tsp sea salt

FOR THE STUFFING
25 g/1 oz/2 tbsp butter
1 small onion, chopped
50 g/2 oz/1 cup fresh white breadcrumbs
2 apples, cored, peeled and chopped
50 g/2 oz/scant ½ cup raisins
finely grated rind of 1 orange
pinch of ground cloves
salt and ground black pepper

1 Preheat the oven to 220°C/425°F/ Gas 7. To make the stuffing, melt the butter in a pan and gently fry the onion for 10 minutes, or until soft and golden in colour. Stir into the remaining stuffing ingredients.

2 Put the pork, rind side down, on a board. Make a horizontal cut between the meat and outer layer of fat, cutting to within 2.5 cm/1 in of the edges to make a pocket.

3 Push the stuffing into the pocket. Roll up lengthways and tie with string. Score the rind at 2 cm/¾ in intervals with a sharp knife.

4 Put the pork joint, rind side down, into a casserole in which it will fit comfortably. Mix the cider and soured cream then pour into the casserole, avoiding the joint. Cook, uncovered, in the oven for 30 minutes.

5 Turn the joint over, so that the rind is on top. Baste with the juices, then sprinkle the rind with sea salt. Cook for 1 hour, basting after 30 minutes.

6 Reduce the oven temperature to 180°C/350°F/Gas 4. Cook for a further 1½ hours. Leave the joint to stand for 20 minutes before carving.

COOK'S TIP: Do not baste during the final 2 hours of roasting so that the crackling becomes crisp.

Pork Roasted with Herbs, Spices & Rum

In the Caribbean, this spicy roast pork is usually barbecued and served on special occasions, as part of a buffet.

Serves 6–8

INGREDIENTS
2 garlic cloves, crushed
45 ml/3 tbsp soy sauce
15 ml/1 tbsp finely chopped celery
25 g/1 oz/2 tbsp chopped spring onion
  (scallion)
7.5 ml/1½ tsp dried thyme
5 ml/1 tsp dried sage
2.5 ml/½ tsp mixed (pumpkin pie) spice
10 ml/2 tsp curry powder
120 ml/4 fl oz/½ cup rum
15 ml/1 tbsp demerara (raw) sugar
1.5 kg/3–3½ lb joint of pork,
  boned and scored
salt and ground black pepper
creamed sweet potato, to serve
spring onion (scallion) curls, to garnish

FOR THE SAUCE
25 g/1 oz/2 tbsp butter or margarine
15 ml/1 tbsp tomato purée (paste)
300 ml/½ pint/1¼ cups chicken stock
15 ml/1 tbsp chopped fresh parsley
15 ml/1 tbsp demerara (raw) sugar
hot pepper sauce, to taste
salt

1 Mix together the garlic, soy sauce, celery, spring onion, thyme, sage, mixed spice, curry powder, rum, demerara sugar and salt and pepper.

2 Open out the pork and slash the meat, without cutting through. Spread the mixture all over the pork, pressing it well into the slashes. Rub the outside of the joint with the mixture and refrigerate overnight.

3 Preheat the oven to 190°C/375°F/Gas 5. Roll up the meat, then tie tightly in several places with strong cotton string to hold it together.

4 Spread a large piece of foil across a roasting tin and place the joint in the centre. Baste the pork with a few spoonfuls of the marinade mixture and wrap the foil around the joint, holding in the marinade.

5 Cook for 1¾ hours, then remove the foil, baste with any remaining marinade and cook for a further 1 hour. Check occasionally that the joint is not drying out and baste with any pan juices.

6 Transfer the pork to a warmed serving dish and leave to stand in a warm place for 15 minutes before serving. Meanwhile make the sauce. Pour the pan juices into a saucepan. Add the butter or margarine.

7 Add the tomato purée, stock, parsley, sugar, pepper sauce and salt. Simmer gently until reduced. Serve the pork sliced, with sweet potato. Garnish with spring onion curls and hand the sauce around separately.

Loin of Pork with Prune Stuffing

Pork and prunes is a popular combination, but the sauce, thickened with crushed ginger biscuits, is a German speciality.

Serves 4

INGREDIENTS

1.5 kg/3–3½ lb cured or smoked loin of pork
75 g/3 oz/about 18 ready-to-eat prunes, finely chopped
45 ml/3 tbsp apple juice or water
75 g/3 oz/1½ cups day-old ginger biscuit (cookie) crumbs
3 cardamom pods
15 ml/1 tbsp sunflower oil
1 onion, chopped
250 ml/8 fl oz/1 cup dry red wine
15 ml/1 tbsp soft dark brown sugar
salt and ground black pepper
buttery fried pitted prunes and apple and leek slices with steamed green cabbage, to serve

2 Put the prunes in a bowl. Spoon over the apple juice or water, then add the biscuit crumbs. Remove the cardamom seeds from their pods and crush. Add to the bowl with salt and pepper. Mix the prune stuffing well and use to fill the pockets in the meat.

1 Preheat the oven to 230°C/450°F/Gas 8. Put the pork, fat side down, on a board. Cut about 3 cm/1¾ in deep along the length to within 1 cm/½ in of the ends, then cut to the left and right to create two pockets in the meat.

3 Tie the pork joint at intervals with string. Heat the oil in a roasting tin and brown the joint over a high heat. Remove the meat and set aside.

4 Add the onion to the tin and fry for 10 minutes, until golden. Return the pork to the tin, pour in the wine and add the sugar and seasoning. Roast for 10 minutes, then reduce the oven temperature to 180°C/350°F/Gas 4 and roast for a further 1 hour and 50 minutes, or until the meat is cooked and golden brown.

5 Remove the joint from the tin and keep warm, covered by a loose tent of foil. Strain the juices into a pan and simmer for 10 minutes, until slightly reduced. Carve the pork and serve with the sauce separately, accompanied by buttery fried pitted prunes and apple and leek slices, together with steamed green cabbage.

Roast Ham

A glazed and roasted whole ham makes an impressive centrepiece for a special party buffet and it is also a classic Christmas dish.

Serves 20–25

INGREDIENTS
4.5 kg/10 lb raw ham, on the bone
2 onions, sliced
1 carrot, sliced
2 celery sticks, sliced
2 bay leaves
1 mace blade
1 cinnamon stick
15 ml/1 tbsp black peppercorns
6 cloves
60 ml/4 tbsp clear honey, warmed
2.5 ml/½ tsp ground cinnamon
pinch of ground cloves

1 First soak the ham in cold water for 3 hours, changing the water from time to time if necessary. Skim any salty scum from the surface of the water and drain the ham thoroughly.

2 The ham must be boiled or baked before roasting. To boil, put the ham, onions, carrot, celery, bay leaves, mace, cinnamon stick, peppercorns and whole cloves into a large saucepan. Fill the pan with fresh water to within 5 cm/2 in of the top. Bring to the boil, cover and simmer for 3 hours 40 minutes, or until the ham is cooked through. Drain and cool.

3 If baking the ham, preheat the oven to 180°C/350°F/Gas 4. Place the drained and dried ham on a large sheet of double-thickness foil. Add the onions, carrot, celery, herbs and spices. Wrap tightly and bake for 3 hours 40 minutes, or until the ham is cooked through. Place the ham on a board and allow to cool.

4 Whether boiled or baked, ease off the rind with a sharp knife and score the fat in diagonal lines to make a diamond pattern. Lightly brush the fat with some of the warmed honey. Sprinkle with the ground cinnamon and ground cloves and roast for 40–50 minutes in a 180°C/350°F/Gas 4 oven.

COOK'S TIP: If you know a reliable butcher or delicatessen, you can buy a whole cooked ham and then glaze and roast it at home, from step 3, to save time.

5 While roasting, baste the fat with more honey to build up a glossy, well-browned crust.

6 To serve, place a ham frill on the bone and rest the ham on a ham stand or large, flat platter.

Cinnamon Crusted Lamb

Racks of lamb are perfect for serving at dinner parties. This version has a deliciously spiced crumb coating.

Serves 6

INGREDIENTS

50 g/2 oz ciabatta bread, broken into pieces
15 ml/1 tbsp drained green peppercorns in
  brine, lightly crushed
15 ml/1 tbsp ground cinnamon
1 garlic clove, crushed
2.5 ml/½ tsp salt
25 g/1 oz/2 tbsp butter, melted
10 ml/2 tsp Dijon mustard
2 racks of lamb, trimmed
60 ml/4 tbsp red wine
400 ml/14 fl oz/1⅔ cups lamb or chicken stock
15 ml/1 tbsp balsamic vinegar
fresh vegetables, to serve

1 Preheat the oven to 220°C/425°F/ Gas 7. Bake the ciabatta for 10 minutes, or until pale and golden.

2 Process in a blender or food processor to make crumbs. Mix the crumbs, peppercorns, cinnamon, garlic and salt in a bowl. Add the butter.

3 Spread mustard over the lamb. Press on the crumb mixture to make a thin even crust. Put the racks in a roasting tin and roast for 30 minutes.

4 Remove the lamb to a carving dish and keep hot under tented foil. Skim the fat off the juices in the roasting tin. Stir in the wine, stock and vinegar.

5 Bring to the boil, stirring in any sediment, then lower the heat and simmer for about 10 minutes to make a rich gravy. Carve the lamb and serve with the gravy and vegetables.

Rack of Lamb with Mustard

To "French" trim a rack of lamb, cut the top 4 cm/1½ in of meat from the thin end of the bones and scrape clean.

Serves 6–8

INGREDIENTS
3 racks of lamb (7–8 ribs each), trimmed of fat, bones "French" trimmed
2–3 garlic cloves
115 g/4 oz (about 4 slices) white or wholemeal (whole-wheat) bread, torn into pieces
25 ml/1½ tbsp fresh thyme leaves
25 ml/1½ tbsp Dijon mustard
ground black pepper
30 ml/2 tbsp olive oil
fresh rosemary, to garnish
new potatoes, to serve

1 Preheat the oven to 220°C/425°F/Gas 7. Trim any remaining fat from the lamb, including the fat covering over the meat.

2 In a food processor fitted with the metal blade, with the machine running, drop the garlic through the feed tube and process until finely chopped. Add the bread, herbs, mustard and a little pepper and process until combined, then gradually pour in the oil.

3 Press the mixture on to the meaty side and ends of the racks, completely covering the surface.

4 Put the racks in a shallow roasting tin, and roast for about 25 minutes for medium-rare or 28–30 minutes for medium. Transfer the meat to a carving board or warmed platter. Cut down between the bones to carve into chops. Serve garnished with rosemary and accompanied by new potatoes.

Field-roasted Lamb

This unusual recipe, originally for mutton slowly roasted over charcoal, comes from the Russian steppes.

Serves 6

INGREDIENTS
1.75 kg/4–4½ lb leg of lamb
4 large garlic cloves, cut into slivers
5 ml/1 tsp whole peppercorns
300 ml/½ pint/1¼ cups natural (plain) yogurt
15 ml/1 tbsp olive oil
15 ml/1 tbsp chopped fresh dill
300 ml/½ pint/1¼ cups lamb or
   vegetable stock
30 ml/2 tbsp lemon juice
roast potatoes, boiled spinach and
   baby carrots, to serve

1 Make slits all over the lamb and insert generous slivers of fresh garlic into the slits.

2 Lightly crush the whole peppercorns in a mortar with a pestle or rolling pin, if preferred. Put the yogurt, oil and crushed peppercorns into a bowl, then add the dill and mix together well.

3 Spread the yogurt paste evenly over the lamb. Put the lamb in a glass dish, cover loosely with foil and then marinate for 1–2 days in the refrigerator, turning it twice.

4 Transfer the lamb to a large roasting tin and let it come back to room temperature. Preheat the oven to 220°C/425°F/Gas 7. Remove the foil. Pour in the lamb or vegetable stock and lemon juice and cook, uncovered, for 20 minutes.

5 Reduce the oven temperature to 180°C/350°F/Gas 4 and continue roasting for a further 1¼–1½ hours, basting occasionally.

6 Remove the lamb from the oven and keep covered with foil in a warm place for 15–20 minutes before carving. Use the juices from the roasting pan to make a gravy and serve with roast potatoes, boiled spinach and baby carrots.

Spiced Roast Lamb

A Turkish version of roast dinner.

Serves 6–8

INGREDIENTS
2.75 kg/6 lb leg of lamb
3–4 large garlic cloves, halved
60 ml/4 tbsp olive oil
10 ml/2 tsp paprika
10 ml/2 tsp Dijon mustard
juice of 1 lemon
2.5 ml/½ tsp dried thyme
2.5 ml/½ tsp dried rosemary
2.5 ml/½ tsp sugar
120 ml/4 fl oz/½ cup white wine
salt and ground black pepper
fresh thyme, to garnish
rice and green salad, to serve

1 Trim the fat from the lamb and make several incisions in the meat with a sharp knife. Press the garlic halves into the slits.

2 Blend together the olive oil, paprika, mustard, lemon juice, herbs, sugar and seasoning and rub this paste all over the meat. Allow to stand in a cool place for 1–2 hours.

3 Preheat the oven to 200°C/400°F/Gas 6. Cook the joint in a roasting tin with the wine for 20 minutes. Reduce the heat to 160°C/325°F/Gas 3 and cook for another 2 hours. Garnish with thyme and serve with rice and salad.

Lamb with Saffron

A tasty Middle Eastern dish.

Serves 6–8

INGREDIENTS
2.75 kg/6 lb leg of lamb
4 garlic cloves, halved
60 ml/4 tbsp olive oil
juice of 1 lemon
2–3 saffron strands, soaked in 15 ml/1 tbsp
   boiling water
5 ml/1 tsp dried mixed herbs
450 g/1 lb potatoes
2 large onions
salt and ground black pepper
fresh parsley, to garnish

1 Make several incisions in the meat and press the garlic halves into the slits. Blend the oil, lemon juice, saffron and herbs. Rub over the meat, then leave to marinate for 2 hours.

2 Preheat the oven to 180°C/350°F/Gas 4. Peel the potatoes. Cut the potatoes and onions into thick slices and layer them in the base of a roasting tin. Place the marinated lamb on top, fat side up. Pour over the marinade.

3 Roast for 2 hours, basting from time to time. Remove the lamb from the oven, cover loosely with foil and leave in a warm place to rest for 10–15 minutes before carving. Serve garnished with fresh parsley.

Roast Leg of Lamb with Beans

Leg of lamb is a favourite Sunday roast and is delicious served with haricot or flageolet beans.

Serves 8–10

INGREDIENTS
2.75–3 kg/6–7 lb leg of lamb
3–4 garlic cloves
olive oil
fresh or dried rosemary leaves
450 g/1 lb dried haricot (navy) or flageolet
   (small cannellini) beans, soaked overnight
1 bay leaf
30 ml/2 tbsp red wine
150 ml/¼ pint/⅔ cup lamb or beef stock
25 g/1 oz/2 tbsp butter
salt and ground black pepper
watercress, to garnish

1 Preheat the oven to 220°C/425°F/ Gas 7. Wipe the lamb with damp kitchen paper and dry the fat covering well. Cut two to three garlic cloves into 10–12 slivers. Make 10–12 slits in the meat and press the garlic into them. Rub with oil, season with salt and pepper and sprinkle with rosemary.

2 Set the lamb on a rack in a shallow roasting tin and put in the oven. After 15 minutes, reduce the heat to 180°C/ 350°F/Gas 4 and continue to roast for 1½–1¾ hours.

3 Meanwhile, rinse the beans and put in a saucepan with enough fresh water to cover generously. Add the remaining garlic and the bay leaf, then bring to the boil. Reduce the heat and simmer for 45 minutes–1 hour, or until tender.

4 Transfer the roast to a board and stand, loosely covered, for 10–15 minutes. Skim off the fat from the cooking juices, then add the wine and stock to the roasting tin. Boil over a medium heat, stirring and scraping the base of the tin, until slightly reduced. Strain into a warmed gravy boat.

5 Drain the beans, discard the bay leaf, then toss the beans with the butter until it melts and season with salt and pepper. Garnish the lamb with watercress and serve with the beans and the sauce.

Mustard-glazed Butterflied Leg of Lamb

Boning and opening out a leg of lamb flat – butterflying – reduces the cooking time by about one-third.

Serves 6–8

INGREDIENTS
115 g/4 oz/¼ cup Dijon mustard
1–2 garlic cloves, finely chopped
30 ml/2 tbsp olive oil
30 ml/2 tbsp lemon juice
30 ml/2 tbsp chopped fresh rosemary or
   15 ml/1 tbsp crumbled dried rosemary
2.25 kg/5–5¼ lb leg of lamb, boned
   and butterflied

2 Add the lamb, secured with skewers, and rub the mixture all over it. Cover the dish and marinate for at least 3 hours. Allow the lamb to return to room temperature before cooking.

1 Combine the mustard, garlic, oil, lemon juice, rosemary, salt and pepper in a shallow, non-metallic dish and mix together well.

3 Preheat the oven to 180°C/350°F/ Gas 4. Place the lamb on a rack in a roasting tin. Spread any remaining mustard mixture over it. Roast for 1¾ hours.

COOK'S TIP: Ask your butcher to bone and butterfly the leg of lamb for you.

4 Transfer to a carving board, cover loosely with foil and keep warm for at least 10 minutes before carving.

Roast Lamb with Apricot, Cinnamon & Cumin Stuffing

Cinnamon and cumin make perfect partners for apricots in the bulgur wheat stuffing in this easy-to-carve joint.

Serves 6–8

INGREDIENTS
75 g/3 oz/½ cup bulgur wheat
30 ml/2 tbsp olive oil
1 small onion, finely chopped
1 garlic clove, crushed
5 ml/1 tsp ground cinnamon
5 ml/1 tsp ground cumin
175 g/6 oz/¾ cup ready-to-eat dried
    apricots, chopped
50 g/2 oz/½ cup pine nuts
1 boned shoulder of lamb,
    about 1.75 kg/4–4½ lb
120 ml/4 fl oz/½ cup
    red wine
120 ml/4 fl oz/½ cup lamb stock
salt and ground black pepper
sprigs of fresh mint, to garnish

1 To make the stuffing, place the bulgur wheat in a bowl and add enough warm water to cover. Leave to soak for 1 hour, then drain off any excess water.

COOK'S TIP: Bulgur wheat, or *burghul*, is a cracked wheat that is often used in Middle Eastern cookery. It can be found in most supermarkets or specialist Middle Eastern shops.

2 Heat the oil in a saucepan. Add the onion and crushed garlic and cook for 5 minutes, until soft. Stir in the cinnamon, cumin, apricots and pine nuts, with salt and pepper to taste. Leave to cool. Preheat the oven to 180°C/350°F/Gas 4.

3 Combine the apricot and onion mixture with the drained bulgur wheat, stirring thoroughly.

4 Open out the shoulder of lamb and spread the stuffing over. Roll up firmly and tie tightly with string.

5 Place in a roasting tin. Roast for 1 hour, then pour the red wine and stock into the roasting tin. Roast for 30 minutes more. Transfer the joint to a heated plate, cover with tented foil and allow the meat to rest for 15–20 minutes before carving.

6 Meanwhile, skim the surface fat from the stock in the roasting tin. Place the tin over a high heat and allow the gravy to bubble for a few minutes, stirring occasionally to incorporate any sediment. Carve the lamb neatly, arrange the slices on a serving platter and pour over the gravy. Serve at once, garnished with mint.

Roast Leg of Lamb with Pesto

Basil is more usually associated with chicken, but the slightly sharp, sweet flavour of pesto perfectly complements lamb.

Serves 6

INGREDIENTS
115 g/4 oz/2 cups fresh basil leaves
4 garlic cloves, coarsely chopped
50 g/2 oz/scant ½ cup pine nuts
150 ml/¼ pint/⅔ cup olive oil
50 g/2 oz/⅔ cup freshly grated
   Parmesan cheese
5 ml/1 tsp salt
2.25 kg/5–5¼ lb leg of lamb

1 To make the pesto, combine the basil, garlic and pine nuts in a food processor and process until finely chopped. With the motor running, gradually add the oil in a steady stream. Scrape the mixture into a bowl. Stir in the Parmesan and salt.

COOK'S TIP: While home-made pesto is delicious, it can be bought ready-made in most supermarkets.

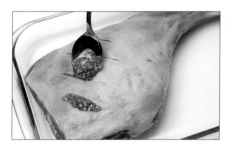

2 Put the lamb in a roasting tin. Make several slits in the meat with a sharp knife and spoon some pesto into each slit. Rub more pesto over the surface of the lamb.

3 Continue patting on the pesto in a thick, even layer. Cover and leave to stand for 2 hours at room temperature, or refrigerate overnight.

4 Preheat the oven to 180°C/350°F/ Gas 4. Place the lamb in the oven and roast for 1 hour 40 minutes–1¾ hours for rare meat and 2–2¼ hours for medium-rare. Turn the lamb from time to time during roasting.

5 Remove the leg of lamb from the oven, cover it loosely with foil, and leave to rest about 15 minutes before carving and serving.

Rib of Beef with Shallots

Roast beef responds best to simple culinary treatments that allow its full flavour to come to the fore.

Serves 8

INGREDIENTS
5 kg/10 lb fore rib of beef
(about 4 ribs), chined
vegetable oil
450 g/1 lb plump shallots, unpeeled
15 g/½ oz/1½ tbsp plain (all-purpose) flour
350 ml/12 fl oz/1½ cups beef stock or
250 ml/8 fl oz/1 cup beef stock and
120 ml/4 fl oz/½ cup red wine
salt and ground black pepper
roast potatoes, to serve (optional)
fresh flat leaf parsley, to garnish

1 Preheat the oven to 180°C/350°F/ Gas 4. If the ends of the rib bones have been left on the joint, scrape them clean, if wished. Rub any exposed bone ends with oil. Season the beef with salt and pepper. Set the joint in a roasting tin, fat side up.

2 Roast the beef uncovered, basting frequently with the cooking juices in the tin, for 3¼–3½ hours for rare meat, 4–4½ hours for medium or 5–5½ hours for well done.

3 Meanwhile, peel off the outer, papery layers from the shallots, leaving at least two layers. Trim the root and stalk ends. About 30 minutes before the beef has finished cooking, put the shallots into the roasting tin around it.

4 When the beef is ready, transfer it to a carving board and set aside to rest for at least 15 minutes. Remove the shallots from the tin and keep warm.

5 Spoon off all but about 30 ml/ 2 tbsp fat from the roasting tin and set the tin over a moderately high heat. When the juices begin to sizzle, stir in the flour. Cook, stirring constantly and scraping the sediment from the base of the tin, for about 1 minute.

6 Gradually stir in the stock or stock and wine mixture. Bring to the boil, stirring constantly, and cook until reduced and thickened. Season with salt and pepper and pour into a gravy boat.

7 Carve the rib of beef. Place on a dish surrounded by the shallots still in their skins (they slip out easily). Serve with roast potatoes, if liked, garnished with fresh flat leaf parsley.

Beef Rib with Onion Sauce

The beef is browned before it is roasted, giving it a distinctive flavour.

Serves 4

INGREDIENTS
1 beef rib with bone, about 1 kg/2¼ lb and
    about 4 cm/1½ in thick, well trimmed of fat
5 ml/1 tsp steak pepper or lightly crushed
    black peppercorns
15 ml/1 tbsp coarse sea salt, crushed
15 ml/1 tbsp unsalted butter
30–45 ml/2–3 tbsp olive oil

FOR THE ONION SAUCE
40 g/1½ oz/3 tbsp unsalted butter
large red onion or 8–10 shallots, sliced
250 ml/8 fl oz/1 cup fruity red wine
250 ml/8 fl oz/1 cup beef or chicken stock
15–30 ml/1–2 tbsp redcurrant jelly or
    seedless raspberry preserve
1.5 ml/¼ tsp dried thyme
salt and ground black pepper

1 Wipe the beef with damp kitchen paper. Mix the steak pepper or crushed peppercorns with the crushed salt and press on to both sides of the meat, coating it completely. Leave to stand, loosely covered, for 30 minutes.

2 To make the sauce, melt the butter in a stainless steel saucepan over a medium heat. Add the onion or shallots and cook for 3–5 minutes, until softened, then add the wine, stock, jelly or preserve and thyme and bring to the boil.

3 Reduce the heat to low and simmer for 30–35 minutes, until the liquid has evaporated and the sauce has thickened. Season with salt and pepper and keep warm.

4 Preheat the oven to 220°C/425°F/ Gas 7. Melt the remaining butter with the oil in a heavy ovenproof frying pan or large flameproof casserole over a high heat.

5 Add the meat and cook for 1–2 minutes, until browned, turn and cook for 1–2 minutes on the other side. Immediately place the pan or casserole in the oven and roast for 8–10 minutes.

6 Transfer the beef to a carving board, cover loosely and leave to stand for 10 minutes. With a knife, loosen the meat from the rib bone, and then carve into thick slices. Serve with the warm onion sauce.

COOK'S TIP: It is possible to expand this recipe for a larger party, but always buy and prepare each beef rib separately, making sure that they are all of the same thickness.

Roast Beef Marinated in Vegetables

This East European dish uses only the best ingredients, including fillet of beef. If you use a sirloin instead, allow a little extra cooking time.

Serves 6

INGREDIENTS

900 g/2 lb fillet or sirloin
2 rindless bacon slices, cut in strips
2 onions, finely chopped
2 carrots, finely chopped
2 parsnips, finely chopped
225 g/8 oz/1 cup celeriac or 4 celery sticks,
    finely diced
2 bay leaves
2.5 ml/½ tsp allspice
5 ml/1 tsp dried thyme
30 ml/2 tbsp chopped fresh
    flat leaf parsley
250 ml/8 fl oz/1 cup red wine vinegar
60 ml/4 tbsp olive oil
50 g/2 oz/4 tbsp butter
2.5 ml/½ tsp sugar
120 ml/4 fl oz/½ cup sour cream
salt and ground black pepper
flat leaf parsley, to garnish

FOR THE DUMPLINGS

6 large potatoes, peeled and quartered
115 g/4 oz/1 cup plain (all-purpose) flour
2 eggs, beaten

1 The day before, lard the beef with strips of bacon and season well with salt and pepper. Place it in a non-metallic bowl and sprinkle the vegetables and bay leaves around it.

2 In another bowl mix together the allspice, thyme, parsley, vinegar and half of the olive oil. Pour over the beef, cover and marinate in the refrigerator for 2–3 hours, basting occasionally.

3 Preheat the oven to 180°C/350°F/ Gas 4. Heat the remaining oil and brown the beef all over. Transfer it to a roasting tin and add the marinade. Dot the top of the meat with butter and sprinkle on the sugar. Roast for 1¼–1½ hours, basting occasionally.

4 To make the dumplings, boil, drain and mash the potatoes. Add the flour and beaten egg. Mix thoroughly.

COOK'S TIP: Larding means to insert strips of pork or bacon into a cut of meat. Insert the strips with a larding needle or your fingers.

5 Turn the potato mixture on to a lightly floured surface and shape into two equal oblong lengths. Place them in a pan of boiling salted water and cook for about 20 minutes. Leave to drain and cool before slicing into individual portions. Set on one side and keep warm.

6 Let the joint stand before carving. Process the vegetables and meat juices in a food processor or blender. Reheat the vegetable purée in a pan and season to taste. Add the sour cream. Carve the beef and serve slices with the sauce and the sliced dumplings. Garnish with the parsley sprigs.

Roast Beef with Porcini & Roasted Sweet Peppers

Substantial, hearty and warming, this is an ideal supper dish to serve for family or friends on cold, dark winter evenings.

Serves 8

INGREDIENTS

1.5 kg/3–3½ lb piece of sirloin
15 ml/1 tbsp olive oil
450 g/1 lb small red (bell) peppers
115 g/4 oz porcini mushrooms
175 g/6 oz thick-sliced pancetta or smoked bacon, cubed
50 g/2 oz/2 tbsp plain (all-purpose) flour
150 ml/¼ pint/⅔ cup full-bodied red wine
300 ml/½ pint/1¼ cups beef stock
30 ml/2 tbsp Marsala
10 ml/2 tsp dried mixed herbs
salt and ground black pepper
roast potatoes, to serve (optional)
fresh flat leaf parsley, to garnish

1 Preheat the oven to 190°C/375°F/ Gas 5. Season the meat well. Heat the olive oil in a large frying pan. When very hot, brown the meat on all sides. Place in a large roasting tin and cook for 1¼ hours.

2 Put the red peppers in the oven to roast for 20 minutes, if small ones are available, or 45 minutes if large ones are used.

3 Near the end of the meat's cooking time, prepare the gravy. Roughly chop the mushroom caps and stems.

4 Heat the frying pan again and add the pancetta or bacon. Cook until the fat runs freely. Add the flour and cook for a few minutes, until browned.

5 Gradually stir in the red wine and the stock. Bring to the boil, stirring. Lower the heat and add the Marsala, herbs and seasoning.

6 Add the mushrooms and heat through. Remove the sirloin from the oven and leave for 10 minutes before carving it. Serve with the peppers, gravy and potatoes, if using.

Beef Wellington

In this delicious version of the famous dish, the beef is coated with a pâté of wild mushrooms before being wrapped in pastry.

Serves 4

INGREDIENTS
675 g/1½ lb fillet steak, tied
15 ml/1 tbsp vegetable oil
350 g/12 oz puff pastry, thawed if frozen
1 egg, beaten, to glaze
ground black pepper

FOR THE PARSLEY PANCAKES
50 g/2 oz/5 tbsp plain (all-purpose) flour
150 ml/¼ pint/⅔ cup milk
1 egg
30 ml/2 tbsp chopped fresh parsley
salt

FOR THE MUSHROOM PATE
2 shallots or 1 small onion, chopped
25 g/1 oz/2 tbsp unsalted butter
450 g/1 lb assorted wild and cultivated
    mushrooms, trimmed and chopped
50 g/2 oz/1 cup fresh white bread, cubed
75 ml/8 tbsp double (heavy) cream
2 egg yolks

1 Preheat the oven to 220°C/425°F/ Gas 7. Season the steak with pepper. Heat the oil in a roasting tin, add the steak and quickly sear to brown all sides. Transfer to the oven and roast for 15 minutes for rare meat, 20 minutes for medium-rare or 25 minutes for well-done meat. Set aside to cool. Reduce the temperature to 190°C/ 375°F/Gas 5.

2 To make the pancakes, beat the flour, salt, half the milk, the egg and parsley together until smooth, then stir in the remaining milk. Heat a greased, non-stick pan and pour in enough batter to coat the base. When set, turn over and cook the other side until lightly browned. With the remaining batter make another three or four.

3 To make the mushroom pâté, fry the shallots or onion in butter to soften. Add the mushrooms and cook until their juices begin to run. Increase the heat and cook briskly so that the juices evaporate.

4 Combine the bread with the cream and egg yolks. Add to the mushrooms and blend to make a smooth paste. Allow to cool.

COOK'S TIP: Beef Wellington can be prepared up to 8 hours in advance and kept at room temperature.

5 Roll out the pastry and cut into a rectangle 35 x 30 cm/14 x 12 in. Place two pancakes on the pastry and spread with mushroom pâté. Place the beef on top and spread over any remaining pâté. Cover with the remaining pancakes. Cut out four squares from the corners of the pastry. Moisten the pastry edges with egg and then wrap them over the meat.

6 Decorate the top with the reserved pastry trimmings, transfer to a baking sheet and rest in a cool place until ready to cook. Brush evenly with beaten egg and cook for about 40 minutes, until golden brown.

Pot-roast Beef with Stout

This heart-warming, rich pot-roast is ideal for a winter's supper. You can use rolled silverside or topside instead of brisket.

Serves 6

INGREDIENTS
30 ml/2 tbsp oil
900 g/2 lb rolled brisket of beef
275 g/10 oz onions, roughly chopped
6 celery sticks, thickly sliced
450 g/1 lb carrots, cut into large chunks
675 g/1½ lb potatoes, cut into
　large chunks
15 g/½ oz/2 tbsp plain (all-purpose) flour
475 ml/16 fl oz/2 cups beef stock
300 ml/½ pint/1¼ cups stout
1 bay leaf
45 ml/3 tbsp chopped fresh thyme
5 ml/1 tsp soft brown sugar
30 ml/2 tbsp wholegrain mustard
15 ml/1 tbsp tomato purée (paste)
salt and ground black pepper

1 Preheat the oven to 180°C/350°F/ Gas 4. Heat the oil in a large flameproof casserole and brown the meat all over until golden. Remove from the pan and drain on kitchen paper. Reduce to medium heat.

2 Add the onions and cook for 4 minutes, or until beginning to soften and turn brown, stirring all the time.

3 Add the celery, carrots and potatoes and cook for 2–3 minutes, or until they are beginning to colour.

4 Add the flour and cook for a further 1 minute. Blend in the stock and stout until combined. Bring to the boil, stirring.

5 Stir in the bay leaf, thyme, sugar, mustard, tomato purée and plenty of seasoning. Place the meat on top, cover tightly and transfer to the oven.

6 Cook for about 2½ hours, or until the vegetables and meat are tender. Adjust the seasoning and add another pinch of sugar, if necessary. To serve, remove the meat and carve into thick slices. Serve with the vegetables and plenty of gravy.

Veal Roast

Veal is often flattened then layered or rolled around fillings. This mixture of veal, bacon, egg and ham as a filling is delicious.

Serves 4–6

INGREDIENTS

1.5 kg/3–3½ lb shoulder of veal or lean
    pork, cut into 2 cm/¾ in slices
225 g/8 oz smoked back bacon slices
175 g/6 oz sliced ham
4 eggs, beaten
45 ml/3 tbsp milk
3 dill pickles, finely diced
115 g/4 oz/½ cup butter
20 g/¾ oz/3 tbsp plain (all-purpose) flour
350 ml/12 fl oz/1½ cups water or
    chicken stock
salt and ground black pepper
baby carrots, runner beans and
    dill pickle slices, to serve

1 Preheat the oven to 180°C/350°F/
Gas 4. Place the veal or pork slices
between two pieces of clear film and
pound or flatten into a regular shape
using a meat mallet or rolling pin until
thin enough to roll.

2 Top each slice of veal or pork with
a layer of bacon and ham. Beat the
eggs in a small pan with the milk and
stir until the mixture is softly
scrambled. Leave to cool and set for
a little while.

3 Place a layer of the scrambled eggs
on top of each slice and spread with a
knife, then sprinkle on the finely diced
dill pickle.

4 Carefully roll up each slice like a
Swiss roll. Tie the rolls securely at
regular intervals with string.

5 Heat the butter in a large
flameproof casserole. Add the meat
rolls and brown on all sides. Remove
the pan from the heat. Remove the
rolls and set aside. Sprinkle the flour
into the pan and stir well.

6 Return the pan to the heat and cook the mixture until pale brown then slowly add half of the water or stock. Return the meat rolls to the pan and bring to the boil, then put the casserole in the oven for 1¾–2 hours, adding the remaining water or stock during cooking if necessary to prevent the veal drying out.

7 When cooked, leave the rolls to stand for 10 minutes, before serving in slices with the gravy and baby carrots, runner beans and dill pickle.

VARIATION: While the veal makes this a good dinner party dish, pork is equally delicious.

Index

This edition is published by Lorenz Books, an imprint of Anness Publishing Ltd, 108 Great Russell Street, London WC1B 3NA info@anness.com www.lorenzbooks.com; www.annesspublishing.com

© Anness Publishing Limited 2014

If you like the images in this book and would like to investigate using them for publishing, promotions or advertising, please visit our website www.practicalpictures.com for more information.

Publisher: Joanna Lorenz
Editor: Valerie Ferguson & Helen Sudell
Series Designer: Bobbie Colgate Stone
Designer: Andrew Heath
Production Controller: Pirong Wang

Recipes contributed by: Catherine Atkinson, Bridget Jones, Carla Capalbo, Carole Clements, Trish Davies, Sarah Edmonds, Rosamund Grant, Rebekah Hassan, Soheila Kimberley, Lesley Mackley, Norma Macmillan, Norma Miller, Sallie Morris, Liz Trigg, Laura Washburn, Steven Wheeler, Elizabeth Wolf-Cohen.

Photography: William Adams-Lingwood, James Duncan, Ian Garlick, Michelle Garrett, Amanda Heywood, Janine Hosegood, David Jordan, Patrick McLeavey, Thomas Odulate.

A CIP catalogue record for this book is available from the British Library

COOK'S NOTES

Bracketed terms are intended for American readers.

For all recipes, quantities are given in both metric and imperial measures and, where appropriate, in standard cups and spoons. Follow one set of measures, but not a mixture, because they are not interchangeable.

Standard spoon and cup measures are level. 1 tsp = 5ml, 1 tbsp = 15ml, 1 cup = 250ml/8fl oz. Australian standard tablespoons are 20ml. Australian readers should use 3 tsp in place of 1 tbsp for measuring small quantities.

American pints are 16fl oz/2 cups. American readers should use 20fl oz/2.5 cups in place of 1 pint when measuring liquids.

Electric oven temperatures in this book are for conventional ovens. When using a fan oven, the temperature will probably need to be reduced by about 10–20°C/20–40°F. Since ovens vary, you should check with your manufacturer's instruction book for guidance.

Medium (US large) eggs are used unless otherwise stated.

PUBLISHER'S NOTE:

Although the advice and information in this book are believed to be accurate and true at the time of going to press, neither the authors nor the publisher can accept any legal responsibility or liability for any errors or omissions that may have been made nor for any inaccuracies nor for any loss, harm or injury that comes about from following instructions or advice in this book.